THE GREAT RACE: FIGHT TO THE FINISH

THE SPACE RACE

JENNIFER MASON

Gareth Stevens
PUBLISHING

Please visit our website, www.garethstevens.com.
For a free color catalog of all our high-quality books,
call toll free 1-800-542-2595 or fax 1-877-542-2596.

CATALOGING-IN-PUBLICATION DATA

Names: Mason, Jennifer.
Title: The space race / Jennifer Mason.
Description: New York : Gareth Stevens Publishing, 2018. | Series: The great race: fight to the finish | Includes index.
Identifiers: ISBN 9781538208229 (pbk.) | ISBN 9781538208205 (library bound) | ISBN 9781538208083 (6 pack)
Subjects: LCSH: Space race--History--Juvenile literature. | Astronautics--United States--History--Juvenile literature. | Astronautics--Soviet Union--History--Juvenile literature. | Space flight--History--Juvenile literature.
Classification: LCC TL793.M37 2018 | DDC 629.4'109046--dc23

Published in 2018 by
Gareth Stevens Publishing
111 East 14th Street, Suite 349
New York, NY 10003

Developed and Produced by Focus Strategic Communications, Inc.

Project Manager: Adrianna Edwards
Editor: Ron Edwards
Layout and Composition: Ruth Dwight
Copy editors: Adrianna Edwards, Francine Geraci
Media Researchers: Adrianna Edwards, Paula Joiner, Maddi Nixon
Proofreader: Francine Geraci
Index: Ron Edwards, Maddi Nixon

PHOTO CREDITS

Credit Abbreviations: **G** Getty; **S** Shutterstock; **WC** Wikimedia Commons

Position on the page: **T:** top, **B:** bottom, **L:** left, **R:** right

Cover: G: Apic; **4-5:** Alex Mit/S; **6:** ESA/Hubble & NASA; **7 TL:** J van Meurs/WC; **7 TR:** iryna1/S; **7 B:** Cezary Stanislawski/S; **8:** Vadim Sadovski/S; **9:** NASA/Marshall Space Flight Center; **10:** Everett Historical/S; **11 L:** Russell Shively/S; **11 R:** Donald Gargano/S; **12:** Fastfission/WC; **13:** Zryzner/S; **14:** Everett Historical/S; **15:** Prisoner labor at construction of Belomorkanal/WC; **16:** NASA/Marshall Space Flight Center; **18-19:** janez volmajer/S; **20:** Georgios Kollidas/S; **22:** NASA/Goddard/Rebecca Roth; **23:** mashurov/S; **24:** NASA/Marshall Space Flight Center; **25:** NASA; **26:** NASA/Marshall Space Flight Center; **27:** Alex Zelenko/WC; **28:** NASA images/S; **29:** AuntSpray/S; **30:** U.S. Navy; **31:** Myroslava/S; **32:** NASA; **33:** studio23/S; **34:** Mikhail Olykainen/S; **35:** NASA; **36:** NASA; **37:** U.S. Air Force photo/Joe Davila; **38:** NASA; **39:** NASA; **40:** Romolo Tavani/S; **41:** Alhovik/S; **42:** Castleski/S; **43:** NASA; **44:** NASA, ESA, Hubble Heritage Team (STScI/AURA).

All rights reserved. No part of this book may be reproduced in any form without permission from the publisher, except by a reviewer.

Printed in the United States of America
CPSIA compliance information: Batch CS17GS: For further information contact Gareth Stevens, New York, New York at 1-800-542-2595.

CONTENTS

Masters of the Universe 4

The World at War 10

What Goes Up 16

Where There's Smoke 24

Wish upon a Star 32

No Place Like Home 40

Timeline 45

Glossary 46

For More Information 47

Index 48

MASTERS OF THE UNIVERSE

A COLD, DARK PLACE

Outer space. It's a place with no air, no life — or at least none that we have found. Space is a cold and endless **expanse** that we can see more clearly at night. How cold is it? Unless you're near a fiery star, the average temperature of space is -455 °F (-271 °C)! But how endless is it?

4

GOING THE DISTANCE

Earth's nearest neighbor, the Moon, is about 238,000 miles away. The farthest planet, Uranus, is about 1.6 billion miles (2.6 billion km) from Earth. The entire solar system — which includes all the planets, moons, comets, asteroids, and meteors swirling around the Sun — is just a dot in the Milky Way Galaxy. Surprisingly, our huge galaxy is just one of thousands of galaxies linked together. These networks form the Virgo Super Cluster, which is still just a dot in the larger **cosmos**.

FAST FACT

The ancient Greeks named our galaxy the Milky Way because, on very clear nights, the stars look like spilled milk across the sky.

UNIMAGINABLE

Space is so large, it is almost impossible to imagine. The distances become so huge that they cannot be measured in miles. Cars travel in miles, but space is too big for cars to travel across. A road trip across the Milky Way in a car speeding 70 miles per hour (113 km/h) would take more than 40 billion years! Light particles, however, can whip across in just 3,200 years.

LIGHT-YEARS

Light zips around at speeds faster than 186,000 miles (299,338 km) per second. The Moon is just over one light-second away. That means it takes about a second for light from the Moon to reach your eyes. The Sun is farther away. Its light needs eight minutes to reach Earth. The distance light can travel in one year is called a **light-year**. In a year, a particle of light can cover 6 trillion miles (10 trillion km)! To put that into perspective, consider the light coming from Proxima Centauri, our closest neighboring star. That light has traveled more than 4 light-years in order to twinkle for you tonight!

When you look at Proxima Centauri, what you see is how the star looked four years ago. It may not even exist anymore!

THE START OF IT ALL

The first telescope was invented in 1608 by Hans Lippershey. Lippershey made eyeglasses to help people see clearer. He designed the telescope for viewing faraway objects. Astronomer Galileo Galilei was the first person to point the telescope at space. His discoveries forever changed the world's understanding of the cosmos and the importance of science!

By combining two telescopes, Hans Lippershey (1570-1619) made the first binoculars. He is shown here in this 1655 portrait.

Galileo Galilei (seen here with his telescope in a 1962 illustration) was the driving force behind the study of **astronomy**.

The twin W.M. Keck Observatory telescopes are the world's largest, each weighing 300 tons (272 metric tons). They are located high above the clouds on Hawaii's Big Island on the 13,796-foot (4,205 m) summit of Maunakea.

SKYWALKERS

Perhaps what is more surprising than all the distances, more stunning than all the dazzling stars, is the fact that we tiny humans have traveled across this unfriendly, frozen, black ocean in the sky. We have sent astronauts to walk on the Moon. We have **probes** circling Mercury, Venus, Saturn, and the Sun! Rovers drive across Mars, gathering samples of soil and other data. The Hubble Space Telescope (HST) is our galactic tourist, sending home the most amazing postcards. Other craft, like *Voyager 1* (launched by **NASA** in 1977), are on a quest to explore deep space. If all goes well, we expect to send people to other planets by the year 2030, starting with Mars.

The Hubble Space Telescope orbits Earth. It was launched on April 1, 1990.

FAST FACT

According to NASA, there are more than half a million objects orbiting Earth. This space junk includes empty rocket boosters, dead satellites, and even some misplaced gloves!

THE LOCKED DOOR

But the door to space was not an easy one to open. It required two of the world's most brilliant minds to pick the lock: Wernher von Braun and Sergei Korolev. These two geniuses competed against each other. They worked on opposite sides of the world, serving countries — the United States and the Soviet Union — that hoped to destroy each other. They raced against an always-ticking clock that was the "space race." Each country wanted to be the first in space so they could be safe from nuclear destruction. This was a race with no award for second place.

FAST FACT

Sergei Korolev worked as the lead Soviet rocket engineer and spacecraft designer during the space race in the 1950s and 1960s. He is considered by many as the father of practical **astronautics**.

Following World War II, Dr. Wernher von Braun (shown here in 1960) arrived in the United States from Germany to continue his rocket development work.

9

THE WORLD AT WAR

WORLD WAR II

In the 1940s, much of Europe was a smoldering, bleeding battlefield. World War II had been raging since 1939. In total, the war claimed the lives of more than 60 million people. The fighting erupted when countries called the Axis Powers invaded their neighbors. This group included Germany, Italy, and Japan. Opposed to them were the Allies: Britain, France, the United States, China, and the Soviet Union. In addition to territorial battles, Adolf Hitler, Chancellor of Germany, tasked his Nazi Party with the extermination of all Jewish people. As a result, millions of Jewish people suffered and died in concentration camps.

Ranks of German soldiers fill Zeppelin Field in Nuremberg during the Nazi Party Congress on September 8, 1938, prior to the breakout of World War II. From a center podium, Adolf Hitler addresses his troops.

BATTLE FOR SURVIVAL

While soldiers in the front lines endured daily horrors on the battlefield, civilians living in towns and cities had to survive day-to-day life. To ensure the armies were well supplied, most foods and common household goods were **rationed**, or limited. Sirens would wail at any time of day or night, sending people to scramble into basements and bomb shelters. Fleets of enemy aircraft flew over cities, dropping thousands of tons of bombs.

WAR RATIONING

Instead of grocery shopping whenever they wanted and buying as much food as they could afford, families could only shop for certain items on certain days. They were also limited on how much they could purchase. Imagine getting only one loaf of bread every two or three weeks, or one bar of soap every month. To "buy" goods, people used ration stamps or tokens instead of cash.

Food and **commodity** ration books and stamps such as these were common during World War II.

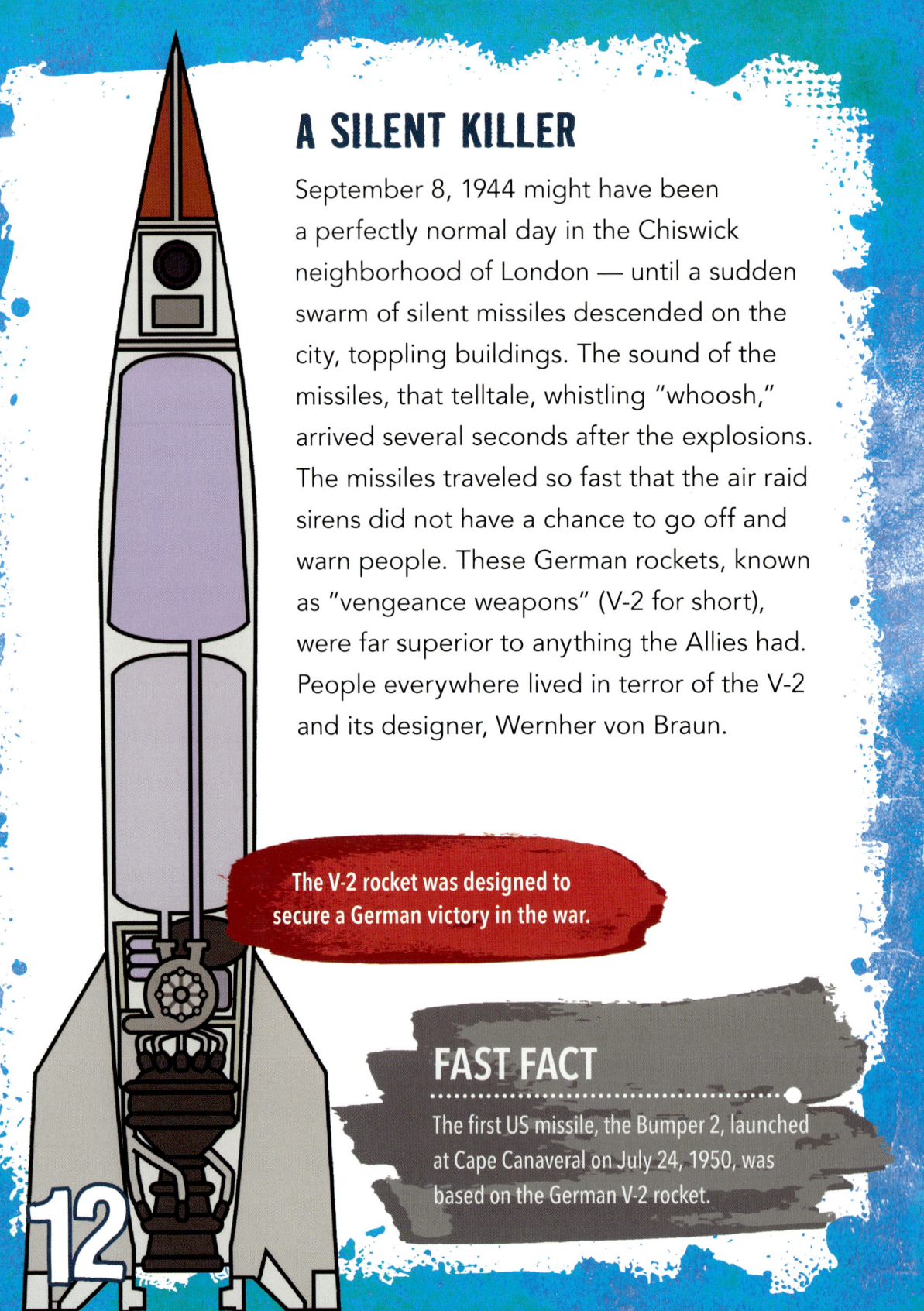

A SILENT KILLER

September 8, 1944 might have been a perfectly normal day in the Chiswick neighborhood of London — until a sudden swarm of silent missiles descended on the city, toppling buildings. The sound of the missiles, that telltale, whistling "whoosh," arrived several seconds after the explosions. The missiles traveled so fast that the air raid sirens did not have a chance to go off and warn people. These German rockets, known as "vengeance weapons" (V-2 for short), were far superior to anything the Allies had. People everywhere lived in terror of the V-2 and its designer, Wernher von Braun.

The V-2 rocket was designed to secure a German victory in the war.

FAST FACT

The first US missile, the Bumper 2, launched at Cape Canaveral on July 24, 1950, was based on the German V-2 rocket.

SCIENCE FICTION, SCIENCE FACTS

Von Braun had been scaring people with rockets ever since he was a boy. When he was 12, von Braun and his younger brother, Magnus, crafted a rocket-powered vehicle by strapping a bunch of fireworks to the back of a cart. People screamed and dove out of the way as the boys shot through town! Young von Braun devoured popular science fiction books by Jules Verne and H.G. Wells. He dreamed of sailing through space the way Ferdinand Magellan sailed around the world in the 1500s. To von Braun, science had the power to make fantasies come true.

This sculpture of the Woking Martian celebrates Woking, UK as the birthplace of H.G. Wells' novel *The War of the Worlds*, published in 1898.

FAST FACT

An adaptation of H.G. Wells's *War of the Worlds* was aired on CBS radio on Halloween in 1938. Directed and narrated by actor and filmmaker Orson Welles, it became famous for allegedly causing mass panic by people who believed that Martians had actually invaded Earth.

FASCINATION WITH FLIGHT

When Sergei Korolev was six, his grandparents took him to an air show to see airplanes spin, whirl, and zoom. He instantly fell in love with flying. By the age of 17, he had designed his own gliders.

Korolev went on to study science and physics. He joined a club of rocket enthusiasts who all dreamed of flying in outer space one day. They stayed up late most nights building or testing rockets. The Russian military recruited Korolev to research new flight technologies.

STRANGE BIRDS

American brothers Wilbur and Orville Wright flew the first motored airplane in 1903. The wingspan measured 40 feet (12 m) across — about the same length as a school bus!

This is the machine in which the Wright Brothers made their first controlled flight, on December 17, 1903.

WRONGLY ACCUSED

Korolev's dreams crumbled when police hauled him away to serve a long sentence in the **Gulag**. In Russia, then called the Soviet Union, the Gulag was a network of prison and labor camps.

Like millions of other Russian prisoners, Korolev was accused of crimes he did not commit. He wrote dozens of letters from the Gulag defending his innocence. Conditions inside the camps were harsh and merciless. Under such suffering, Korolev must have thought his old life a fairy tale.

As the end of the war drew closer in 1945, both von Braun and Korolev were fighting to stay alive.

THE GULAG

The Gulag labor camps operated in the Soviet Union between the 1930s and 1950s. Millions of people were imprisoned in these camps, and many died from overwork, illness, or other causes. Experts estimate that 5 million to 10 million people died in the Gulag.

Prisoners labor to construct the White Sea Canal, northeast of Leningrad (now St. Petersburg, Russia). Many thousands of Gulag prisoners died during the building of the canal (1931–1933).

WHAT GOES UP

As Germany began to lose the war, Nazi leaders ordered the complete destruction of all V-2 factories, equipment, and technical plans. They did not want their enemies to have German rocket technology. This decision also meant von Braun and his team had to be killed so that Allied enemies could not benefit from his knowledge. Von Braun and his team hid in a forest to avoid capture by the Soviets.

By the end of April 1945, Allied troops had captured most of Germany. Von Braun and his team surrendered to American troops. The fighting in Europe was soon over.

In Russia, Korolev's desperate pleas were finally answered. He was released from prison. The space race was about to begin.

Dr. Wernher von Braun (center, arm in cast) surrenders to the US Army in Ruette, Bavaria, on May 2, 1945.

GERMAN SCIENTISTS

The German V-2 rockets were slow and not very accurate, but they pointed the way to future rocket development. The end of fighting led to a scramble among the Allies to capture as many German scientists and their documents as possible. The United States rounded up more than 1,500 German engineers and scientists, including Wernher von Braun, and put them to work developing rockets. This team would soon become the core of NASA and the US space race.

SOVIET ROCKETS

Like their allies, the Soviet Union sent groups to search Germany for rocket secrets and the scientists and engineers who had helped develop the V-2 rocket program. The Soviet military swiftly put Korolev and their captured German rocketeers to work building super-fast, long-range rockets. Soon, Korolev's team had improved on the V-2 technology and produced the R-7 rocket.

FAST FACT

It was the R-7 that made history when it carried *Sputnik 1* into orbit on October 4, 1957.

UNBREAKABLE LAWS

Regardless of their different circumstances at the start of the space race, von Braun and Korolev had the same laws of nature to contend with. If they were going to reach the finish line in the race to space, they would need to overcome **gravity**. Gravity is a force or a mutual pull between objects. Earth possesses gravity; so does an apple. Earth's gravity pulls on the apple just as the apple's gravity pulls on Earth. But because Earth is so huge, its gravity is stronger and pulls harder. As a result, apples fall to the ground when their stems break from trees.

> The Sun, Earth, and Moon are held together by gravity. Gravity is the force that both pulls them together and keeps them from floating away.

THE SOLAR SYSTEM

Because the Sun is so big, its gravity is very powerful. The Sun's gravity holds 8 planets, 5 dwarf planets, 181 moons, more than 3,000 comets, and over half a million asteroids in constant orbit. Asteroids are lumps of rock. When they pass through Earth's atmosphere, they are called meteors or shooting stars. Comets are lumps of frozen gas and dust. As heat from the Sun thaws a comet, ghostly, glowing tails streak behind it.

FLOAT OR FALL

If you drop something, it crashes to the ground. We all know that. But why don't things float in the air? In 1665, Isaac Newton wondered precisely that. The young genius proposed his theory of gravity, or the pulling force. He calculated that gravity weakened over distance. The farther away you traveled from Earth, the less you felt its gravitational pull, until finally, there is no pull whatsoever.

Newton used his gravitational theory to establish a precise set of rules to explain and predict how everything in the universe moved. You might think it would take thousands of rules. Actually, Newton needed only three rules — which he called the Laws of Motion.

Sir Isaac Newton (1643-1727) is shown in an 1837 painting.

OBEY THE LAW

Newton's First Law of Motion says that objects will forever do whatever they are currently doing unless another force interferes. In other words, a motionless ball will remain where it is unless you kick it. Likewise, a ball whooshing through the air would do that forever, if gravity didn't pull it back down to the ground. The Second Law says that if two objects are pushed with the same force, the one with less mass will go faster. And the Third Law predicts that for any action, there is an equal and opposite reaction.

FAST FACT

Scientists calculate that the universe is continually expanding. A mysterious force called Dark Energy seems to be pushing the universe so fast that gravity is losing its grip.

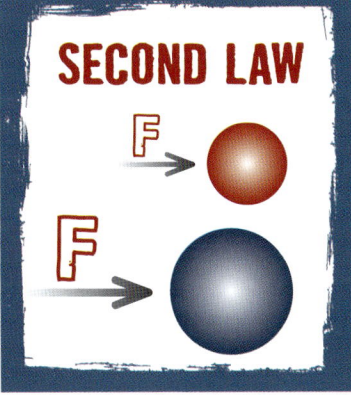

PUZZLES AND CONUNDRUMS

Newton's laws presented Korolev and von Braun with a tangled puzzle. All rockets in motion eventually slowed down because of gravity and air friction. A small rocket could travel faster than a big one, but it could not hold all the fuel it needs to travel beyond the reach of Earth's gravity. But a big rocket with a lot of fuel would be heavier, causing the Earth to pull harder on it, so it could not fly as far. And no matter how hard the fuel pushed a rocket up, gravity would apply an equal and opposite pull back down.

If either Korolev or von Braun was going to reach outer space, they were going to have to do the impossible and break the laws of nature — or maybe they could simply outsmart them!

Dr. Neil deGrasse Tyson (seen here in 2014 during his visit to NASA's Goddard Space Flight Center) is one of the world's leading astrophysicists and cosmologists. He studies the laws of movements in space and the origin of the universe. He has helped millions of people understand the complexities of outer space.

GUNNING DOWN SOLUTIONS

To solve the complex puzzle, both Korolev and von Braun designed their rockets like guns. They decided to point the barrel of their rocket "guns" at the ground, not the sky. They would shoot a bullet of fiery fuel at the Earth and allow the equal–opposite reaction to push the rocket into space.

Despite overcoming the huge barriers science threw in their path, both men faced a seemingly immovable obstacle: lack of interest. The military leaders wanted missiles for warfare, not space travel. The public saw no point in exploring space. It was just a big, cold, empty place. Why bother?

Guns create a sudden explosion in a tight space. The explosion shoves the bullet out of the barrel. The bullet zooms in one direction while an equal and opposite force zooms behind it in the opposite direction. This pushback is called **recoil**.

WHERE THERE'S SMOKE

DO OR DIE

Sergei Korolev knew from his time in the Gulag how unforgiving his government could be if he failed to reconstruct a V-2. He built copies of von Braun's V-2 rockets and tested them. Over and over, the test missiles failed. Sometimes they exploded on the launchpad; other times, they blew up moments after takeoff. Worried these failures would result in punishment, Korolev defied his orders and drew up designs for his very own long-range missile — the R-7.

REALLY LONG RANGE

NASA's *Voyager 1* space probe travels at speeds around 38,000 miles (61,155 km) per hour — that's 11 miles (18 km) per second! In about 40 years, it has traveled beyond the solar system, or roughly 12 billion miles (19 billion km) from Earth (as of 2015).

Voyager 1 was launched on September 5, 1977. It still communicates with the Deep Space Network to receive routine commands and to return data. As of June 2016, *Voyager* was the spacecraft farthest from Earth.

THE MAGICIAN

No matter how many meetings von Braun scheduled with military officials, he failed to arouse any interest in space travel. He decided to appeal directly to the American people and their historic attraction to uncharted frontiers. At this time, there was one man in the whole country with the power to plug an idea into just about everyone's imagination: Walt Disney. In the late 1920s, Disney had created the hugely popular cartoon character, Mickey Mouse, through the world's first animated cartoon with sound. Like a magician, Disney wowed audiences with his full-length animated movies, including *Snow White and the Seven Dwarfs*, *Pinocchio*, *Dumbo*, and *Bambi*. In 1950 — the same year NASA successfully launched the Bumper 2 rocket — Disney released *Cinderella*.

In the 1950s, von Braun worked as a technical director on three Disney films about space exploration. Here, von Braun (right), is pictured with Walt Disney in 1954.

THE FINAL FRONTIER

In 1955, Disney put von Braun on television. Before an audience of 40 million viewers, von Braun shared his excitement for space travel and how it could be accomplished. Disney provided short animated cartoons to help people grasp the complex science of physics and rocketry. Von Braun also revealed a model for the space rocket he yearned to build. On the top of a huge missile, von Braun attached a sleek glider — similar to the ones he designed as a boy. The rocket would launch the glider into space and then break away. Like a sleek airplane, the glider could orbit Earth before smoothly returning its astronaut crew to the ground. The broadcast was a hit. America turned space crazy!

Dr. Wernher von Braun (right) and Dr. Ernst Stuhlinger discuss Mars missions at the Walt Disney Studios in California. As a part of the Disney Tomorrowland series on the exploration of space, nuclear-electric vehicles were shown in the last of three television films, entitled *Mars and Beyond*, which first aired in December 1957.

AS SEEN ON TV

Von Braun's broadcast was also seen by Korolev in Russia. Assuming von Braun was ahead in developing a spacecraft, Korolev rushed to finish his R-7. A year later, Korolev admired his enormous 300-ton (272 metric ton) beast, which was equipped with rocket engines capable of about 300 tons of thrust! After much persuasion, Korolev convinced the Russian leader, Nikita Krushchev, to use the R-7 to put a satellite in space rather than a nuclear bomb on US soil. Korolev gave his team of engineers the design for *"Object D,"* a sophisticated satellite able to gather all sorts of data from outer space.

A model of the R-7 rocket is on display at the All Russian Exhibition Center in Moscow, Russia.

TWO ROCKETS, ONE WINNER

A year later, multiple tests of the R-7 failed, ending in huge explosions. The engineers determined the R-7 was too big and bulky to fly. It needed to slim down, and fast — because von Braun had successfully tested his Jupiter-C rocket. Less powerful than the R-7, the Jupiter still managed to break all previous altitude records, reaching heights of about 650 miles (1,046 km) in late 1956. It could easily carry a satellite into space. In less than 30 days, Korolev's team finished their rebuild and produced the *Sputnik* **prototype**, a beach ball-size metal sphere with four metal rods sticking out like a comet's tail. *Sputnik* ("Fellow Traveler") was equipped with a simple radio transmitter that would beep.

MARS ROVERS

The hardest part of getting the *Opportunity*, *Spirit*, and *Curiosity* rovers to Mars was the landing. Scientists call it "seven minutes of terror." The rover must slow down from about 13,000 miles per hour (20,921 km/h), eject parachutes, fire up guidance rockets, and land on all six wheels in seven minutes — or crash and burn!

Curiosity rover explores the surface of Mars.

SPUTNIK

On October 4, 1957, at 10:28 p.m., an R-7 rocket flew beyond the dome of Earth's atmosphere. At 12:03 a.m., *Sputnik 1* popped out of the rocket and began a circular orbit around the blue planet, calling, "Beep, beep, beep." Anyone with a radio tuner could hear *Sputnik*'s song. In Russia, people celebrated. In America, they panicked. Von Braun was devastated. Not only did Russia have a rocket able to carry nuclear weapons across the ocean, but also, the Russians could be spying on the United States from space! Surely, the US military had their own satellite ready to go. Surely, they had a plan to knock *Sputnik* from the sky.

If only that were true.

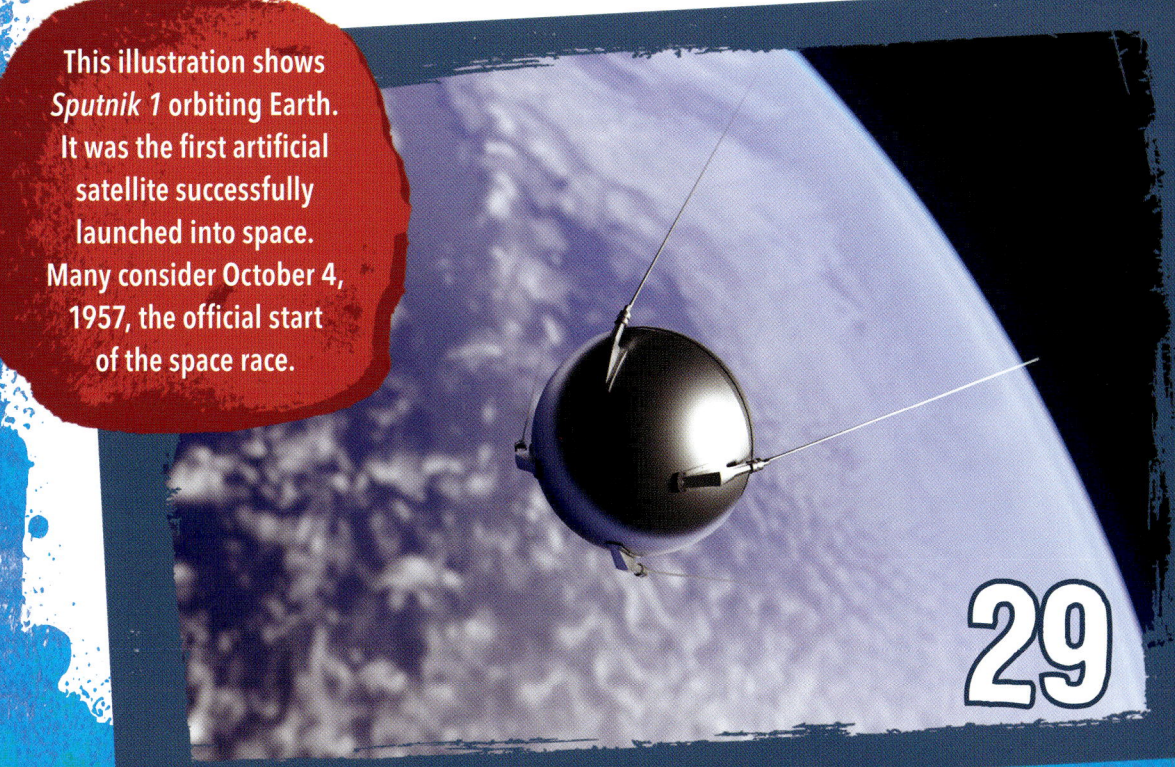

This illustration shows *Sputnik 1* orbiting Earth. It was the first artificial satellite successfully launched into space. Many consider October 4, 1957, the official start of the space race.

HOLDING A GRUDGE

Despite von Braun's successful test of the Jupiter-C rocket, the US military did not have a space-ready vehicle, let alone an orbital satellite. Some officials still held a grudge against von Braun. They did not want a former Nazi leading America into space. As a result, the US Navy led the slow and steady effort to construct its own space-capable rocket. *Sputnik*'s successful launch sent them scrambling to finish their Vanguard rocket. With hundreds of television cameras rolling, the Vanguard TV3 attempted a journey into space just two months after *Sputnik*'s launch. It bumped a few feet off the ground before collapsing in a ball of fire.

On December 6, 1957, the Vanguard rocket was launched. A malfunction caused the vehicle to lose thrust after two seconds and fall to the ground, exploding.

FAST FACT

Scientists estimate the universe is nearly 14 billion years old. Evidence suggests it formed from a massive explosion known as the Big Bang. There was actually no "bang" at all because sound cannot travel in space. Sound needs air to travel.

DOGS IN SPACE

Flopnik! Oopsnik! Dudnik! Kaputnik! Headlines like these mocked the pitiful Vanguard. The military finally gave von Braun the go-ahead. Meanwhile, Korolev successfully launched the first dog into space. Laika survived the first five hours of her space journey around Earth. In the wake of the news, von Braun resolved to outdo his competitor once and for all. He prepared to launch a Jupiter rocket carrying an *Explorer 1* satellite. His rocket was so light and fast that it could carry a state-of-the-art data collector. Von Braun's creation would do more than beep when it arrived in outer space!

This 1987 North Korean stamp marked the 30th anniversary of the first space flight with a dog. Laika, the space dog, became a hero worldwide.

FAST FACT

Throughout most of the space race, von Braun had no idea who the Soviets' space magician was. While everything von Braun developed wound up on television, Korolev's work was kept top-secret. Even the Soviet people did not know Korolev existed.

WISH UPON A STAR

Just four months after *Sputnik*, on January 31, 1958, von Braun launched Explorer 1 into space. President Dwight D. Eisenhower signed a public order creating the National **Aeronautics** and Space Administration, or NASA, that same year. The agency was created solely for space exploration. At the same time that Korolev began a nationwide hunt for cosmonauts, NASA began selecting astronauts. For a moment, the space race was tied!

On April 9, 1959, NASA introduced its first astronauts, known as the Mercury 7. They are pictured here: (front row, left to right) Wally Schirra, Deke Slayton, John Glenn, and Scott Carpenter; (back row) Alan Shepard, Gus Grissom, and Gordon Cooper.

SHOCKING PHOTOS

To the surprise of the whole world, Korolev sent a probe all the way to the Moon! In October 1959, *Luna 3* snapped photos of the Moon's never-before-seen dark side. Hard on the heels of this success, Korolev then built a space capsule designed to carry a man to space and back. *Vostok* ("East") resembled a large bubble. It had many little guidance rockets, or **thrusters**, to steer it in space, which Korolev's team would operate by remote control. The engineers expected the capsule's shell to reach temperatures of 6,000 °F (3,315 °C) or more when it reentered Earth's atmosphere — in other words, nearly as hot as the Sun's surface!

ATMOSPHERE

Earth's atmosphere is a layer of gases, including nitrogen and oxygen, that surrounds our planet. Besides holding the oxygen we breathe, the atmosphere blocks some harmful solar rays, and it traps the heat we need to live comfortably.

atmosphere

Without its atmosphere, Earth would be uninhabitable.

DOUBLE TROUBLE

Back in the United States, von Braun struggled to build a rocket big and powerful enough to carry a person into space. In 1957 and 1958, his latest Atlas model blew up on every test run. Von Braun resurrected an old battle rocket called Redstone. Updating and outfitting the old Redstone was preferable to testing any more Atlas rockets. Besides rocket troubles, the team assembling the *Mercury* capsule for the astronauts fell far behind schedule when the capsule would not fit atop a missile.

In 1960, Korolev dazzled the world again when another Vostok launch carried two dogs, Belka and Strelka, into space and brought them safely home. The Soviets were mastering space travel fast.

This replica of a Vostok rocket is on display at the All Russia Exhibition Hall in Moscow. The Vostok rocket family was derived from the earlier R-7 series.

34

MAN IN SPACE

In the early morning hours of April 12, 1961, cosmonaut Yuri Gagarin was strapped into the *Vostok 1* space capsule. He sang to calm his nerves while Korolev and his team of scientists prepared to hurl him into outer space. At 9:06 am, the Vostok-K rocket beneath him blasted off. For three minutes, the cosmonaut traveled at 17,000 miles per hour (27,359 km). Five minutes after launch, he became the first person to gaze at Earth from outer space. Gagarin orbited the entire planet once, traveling 25,000 miles (40,233 km).

Yuri Gagarin, seen here on April 1, 1961, preparing for his historic flight, was the first human in space. Unlike the early US human spaceflight programs, Gagarin did not land inside a capsule, but was ejected and landed by parachute.

FAST FACT

Where does Earth's atmosphere end and space begin? The Karman line is 62 miles (100 km) above sea level. This is the height where the atmosphere becomes too thin to support aeronautic flight.

35

REFUSING DEFEAT

Von Braun and the entire NASA team were determined to keep pace with the Soviet space program. Twenty-three days after Gagarin's historic flight, they launched astronaut Alan Shepard. Shepard's flight might have only nipped just over 10 miles (16 km) into space, but it enabled the United States to keep a toehold in the race. Tired of duplicating what the Soviets had already perfected, President John F. Kennedy delivered an exciting announcement in the early 1960s. He declared that the United States would land a man on the Moon before the decade was over. In response, NASA initiated the Apollo Program.

> On May 25, 1961, less than three weeks after Shepard's historic flight, President John F. Kennedy addressed Congress, stating that the United States would send a man to the Moon and return him safely to Earth before the decade was out.

EXPLOSIVE ISSUES

In order to lift a crew of astronauts into space, von Braun had to find ways to outsmart gravity yet again. By 1964, he had completed designs for the Saturn V rocket. Standing 350 feet (106 m) tall and weighing 6.5 million pounds (3 million kg), it was a giant. Its five F-1 engines were super-sized versions of the fireworks he mounted on a cart when he was a boy. The first stage of the rocket alone produced nearly 8 million pounds (4 million kg) of thrust. The rockets also exploded often. The fuel system injected a mix of liquid oxygen and kerosene into the F-1. The great engines sucked up over 15,000 gallons (6,000 L) of fuel per minute — enough to fill a small swimming pool. Too much or too little of either ingredient, and F-1 would become a fireball!

DELTA IV HEAVY

The Saturn V rocket was retired from use in 1973. To date, the fastest rocket in use is the Delta IV Heavy. It generates about 2.1 million pounds (1 million kg) of thrust at launch — nowhere near the Saturn V's earthshaking record!

The Delta IV Heavy rocket is shown at a launch on August 28, 2013. The first launch was in 2004. It is the largest rocket ever launched from the West Coast of the United States.

A HEART TOO FRAIL

In mid-March 1965, cosmonaut Alexey Leonov exited his space capsule and performed the first-ever spacewalk. On the heels of that triumph, Korolev sent probes to the Sun and Venus. He launched the first woman cosmonaut, Valentina Tereshkova, into space in June 1963. He designed the N-1 rocket and a new capsule, *Soyuz*, to carry multiple cosmonauts to the Moon.

Sergei Korolev's time in the Gulag left him in poor health, and after several heart attacks, he died during surgery in January 1966, his heart too frail to survive anesthesia.

FLATs

The First Lady Astronaut Trainees (FLATs) consisted of 13 female pilots. They endured and passed the same grueling physical and mental tests given to the men applying to become astronauts. However, they were denied the chance to fly because of their gender.

The FLATs (pictured here in this 1995 photograph) were also known as the Mercury 13. Although FLATs was never an official NASA program, the commitment of these women paved the way for others who followed.

FAST FACT
Sally Ride became the US's first female astronaut in June 1983.

FALLEN HEROS

Following his death, Korolev's identity was finally released. He received a full state funeral and was celebrated as a national hero among the Russian people. Von Braun at last discovered the identity of his longtime rival.

In the shadow of Korolev's death, both space programs experienced devastating tragedies. On January 27, 1967, three astronauts were killed when a fire flared inside their *Apollo 1* capsule. They died on the launchpad before the rocket ever took off. A few months later, a test flight of the Soyuz rocket suffered from multiple mechanical malfunctions, and the cosmonaut, Vladimir Komarov, died.

Was it time to give up on a potentially impossible dream cooked up by two young and imaginative boys?

On January 27, 1967, astronauts Gus Grissom, Ed White, and Roger Chaffee (left to right) were preparing for what was to be the first manned Apollo flight. During the testing, a fire broke out in their capsule, and all three were killed.

NO PLACE LIKE HOME

HAPPY HOLIDAYS

In the final days of December 1968, Frank Borman, James Lovell, and William Anders blasted off into space. The Apollo 8 crew traveled well over a half million miles (800,000 km) to and from the Moon and 10 lunar orbits. They spent Christmas Eve gliding 70 miles (113 km) over the lunar surface inside the *Gemini* spacecraft and made a television broadcast, which was the most-watched television program ever up to that time. These three Americans were the first humans to orbit the Moon, and the first to see Earth rise like a blue sun over the Moon's horizon. Von Braun marked July 16, 1969, on his calendar for the next launch. If all went well, people were going to walk on the Moon.

This illustration shows blue Earth rising from behind the Moon's surface.

STUMBLING AT THE FINISH LINE

Resolved to win the space race once and for all, the Soviet space program tested Korolev's N-1 rocket in early July. Whereas the Saturn V used only five engines, the N-1 relied on 30! The N-1 shot powerfully into the air, but a single bolt was sucked into a fuel pump. The rocket exploded with almost the force of a nuclear bomb. It scattered debris over six miles (10 km)! It was the largest artificial non-nuclear explosion in history. The catastrophe essentially ended Soviet efforts to land people on the Moon.

THE MOON

Scientists think the Moon formed when a Mars-sized planet smashed into Earth a few billion years ago. Over time, the Moon has drifted farther away. Every year, it scoots another 1.5 inches (4 cm) away from Earth.

The Moon is Earth's closest neighbor in space. Still, it is about 239,000 miles (384,400 km) away.

THE LAUNCH SEEN AROUND THE WORLD

On July 16, 1969, a million people gathered at Cape Canaveral, Florida to watch the launch of the Apollo 11 space mission to the Moon. Half a billion people tuned in to watch live on their televisions. The Saturn V rocket was so powerful and so loud, it registered on earthquake sensors across the country! On July 20, 1969, Michael Collins carefully lowered the lunar module. His fellow astronauts Neil Armstrong and Edwin "Buzz" Aldrin stepped out onto the Moon's surface.

"One small step for man, one giant leap for mankind," Armstrong said to the world as he stepped off the bottom rung of the ladder.

FALLING STARS

In the decades after the Moon landing, NASA replaced missiles and capsules with powerful shuttles. Most of the Space Shuttle missions were huge successes for scientific research or testing new technology and equipment. A few ended in tragic disasters. In 1986, the shuttle *Challenger* exploded on takeoff while carrying a crew of seven. Then, in 2003, *Columbia* did not survive reentry to Earth's atmosphere after its space mission. NASA retired the Space Shuttle program in 2011.

In more recent years, rockets carrying equipment **payloads** have sometimes gone up in smoke — proof that the door to space is never wide open. But successes have overwhelmingly outnumbered failures.

On June 28, 2015, a Falcon 9 rocket exploded in the air soon after takeoff (shown here) due to a faulty strut. On September 1, 2016, the Falcon 9, carrying a communications satellite (*Amos 6*) into space, mysteriously exploded while fueling.

INFINITY AND BEYOND

The end of NASA's three-decade Space Shuttle program essentially opened the realm of space travel to other countries — and companies — around the world. The launch of the International Space Station project in 1998 began a new era of cooperation among the world's scientists.

Now, innovative businesses are embarking on a whole new race into the dark, cold realm of space. Will they mine water or minerals from far-off planets? Will they establish colonies on Mars? Will they finally find other forms of life in the universe? Only time will tell, but this we know for certain — humanity's desire to explore space is as vast as the star-studded universe.

On March 17, 2014, astronomers captured images of stars being born 6,400 light-years away, a small portion of the Monkey Head Nebula, to celebrate the launch of NASA's Hubble Space Telescope.

TIMELINE

1944: Sergei Korolev is released from his prison sentence.

1945: Wernher von Braun relocates to the US.

1957: Soviets successfully put *Sputnik 1* in orbit around Earth; Laika becomes the first "space dog."

1958: US sends *Explorer 1* into orbit; NASA is created.

1959: *Luna 3* orbits the Moon and takes pictures of its unseen dark side.

1961: Yuri Gagarin blasts off to become the first person in space and to orbit Earth.

1961: Alan Shepard makes a suborbital spaceflight.

1963: Valentina Tereshkova becomes the first woman in space.

1965: Alexey Leonov performs the first spacewalk outside a spacecraft.

1966: Korolev dies during surgery.

1967: *Apollo 1* capsule catches fire, killing astronauts Gus Grissom, Ed White, and Roger Chaffee.

1967: Vladimir Komarov dies upon reentry in the *Soyuz 1* capsule.

1969: Neil Armstrong and Edwin "Buzz" Aldrin are the first humans to walk on the Moon.

1998: Launch of International Space Station.

GLOSSARY

aeronautics the science that deals with airplanes and flying.

astronautics the science of constructing and operating spacecraft.

astronomy the study of stars, planets, and other objects in outer space.

commodity an article that is bought and sold in commerce.

cosmos the orderly universe.

expanse a wide space, area, or stretch.

gravity the force or mutual pull between objects.

Gulag a network of prison and labor camps in the former Soviet Union.

light-year the distance light can travel in one year.

NASA the US National Aeronautics and Space Administration.

payload something carried by a vehicle in addition to what is necessary for its operation.

probe a device used to send back information, especially from outer space.

prototype an original model on which something is patterned.

rationing an allowance of food or other goods during times of shortage.

recoil the pushback in response to a force, such as a gun firing.

thrusters small guidance rockets that steer a space capsule.

FOR MORE INFORMATION

Books

Berger, M. *Discovering Mars: The Amazing Story of the Red Planet*. New York: Scholastic, 2015.

Flitcroft, I. and Spencer, B. *Journey by Starlight: A Time Traveler's Guide to Life, the Universe, and Everything*. New York: One Peace Books, 2013.

Macy, Sue. *Sally Ride: Life on a Mission*. New York: Simon & Schuster, 2014.

Throp, Claire. *A Visit to a Space Station*. Mankato, MN: Capstone, 2014.

Websites

Amazing Space: Space Telescope Education Program:
http://amazingspace.org/

American Museum of Natural History:
http://www.amnh.org/explore/ology

NASA Kids' Club:
https://www.nasa.gov/kidsclub/index.html

NASA Space Place:
http://spaceplace.nasa.gov/

Publisher's note to educators and parents: Our editors have carefully reviewed these websites to ensure that they are suitable for students. Many websites change frequently, however, and we cannot guarantee that a site's future contents will continue to meet our high standards of quality and educational value. Be advised that students should be closely supervised whenever they access the Internet.

INDEX

Aldrin, Edwin "Buzz," 42
Anders, William, 40
Apollo Program, 36, 39, 40, 42
Armstrong, Neil, 42
astronautics, 9, 35
astronomy, 7, 44
Borman, Frank, 40
Collins, Michael, 42
Disney, Walt, 25, 26
Eisenhower, Dwight D., 32
Gagarin, Yuri, 35, 36
Galilei, Galileo, 7
gravity, 18, 19, 20, 21, 22
Gulag, 14, 15, 24, 38
Hubble Space Telescope, 8, 44
International Space Station, 44
Kennedy, John F., 36
Komarov, Vladimir, 39
Korolev, Sergei, 9, 14, 15, 16, 17, 18, 22, 23, 24, 27, 28, 31, 32, 33, 34, 35, 38, 39, 41
Krushchev, Nikita, 27
Laika, 31
Leonov, Alexey, 38
Lovell, James, 40
light-year, 6, 44
Lippershey, Hans, 7
Magellan, Ferdinand, 13
Mercury (planet) 8
Mercury 7, 32
Mercury 13, 38
Mercury capsule, 38
NASA, 8, 17, 22, 24, 25, 32, 36, 38, 43, 44
Newton, Isaac, 20, 21, 22
rationing, 11
Ride, Sally, 38
Shepard, Alan, 32, 36
Space Shuttle, 43, 44
Sputnik, 17, 28, 29, 30, 32
telescopes, 7, 8, 44
Tereshkova, Valentina, 38
Tyson, Neil deGrasse, 22
Verne, Jules, 13
von Braun, Wernher, 9, 12, 13, 15, 16, 17, 18, 22, 23, 24, 25, 26, 27, 28, 29, 30, 31, 32, 34, 36, 37, 39, 40
Voyager 1, 8, 24
Wells, H.G., 13
World War II, 9, 10, 11, 14
Wright Brothers, 14